# It's Me Brooklyn!

written by Ruth Coyne

Illustrated by Cole Houser

Based on a true story

ISBN:

eBook: 979-8-89604-384-3
Paperback: 979-8-89604-385-0
Hardcover: 979-8-89604-419-2

# Dedication

This book is dedicated to Brooklyn and all families affected by cancer.

Proceeds from the sale of this book will be donated to support cancer awareness and research.

# About the Author

Ruth wrote this book after experiencing the heartbreaking cancer diagnosis of her two-year-old nephew and seeing its effect on his family.

Brooklyn was four years old at the time of the diagnosis. This book was written to share her journey of understanding how her role in the family changed, and to help other siblings of cancer patients better understand their own feelings.

Ruth is retired and lives in oregon with her husband.

# About the Illustrator

Cole Houser is currently a sophomore at the University of Minnesota School of Design. He agreed to illustrate this book both to help siblings of cancer patients and to grow his own creative abilities.

When he is not living in Minneapolis, MN, for school, he resides in Oregon with his family.

# Acknowledgment

We are deeply grateful to the angels among us who carried our family through this journey with prayers, love, and unwavering support. From Jerry and Marge in New York, to friends and family in Kansas and Oregon, and to Eileen, Janet, Monica, Andrea, and the entire ministry in Oregon—you have our eternal gratitude. Your strength, faith, and compassion will always be remembered.

To the medical teams at children's hospitals across the world: your tireless dedication to easing suffering and bringing comfort to families is nothing short of heroic. There is a special place in heaven for those who devote their lives to caring for the most vulnerable.

To the parents and families who face the unthinkable—may God grant you peace and courage. And to those walking this path without support, please know you are not alone. We see you, we honor you, and we lift you up in prayer.

A heartfelt thank you to the exceptional editorial team at writerCosmos, whose professionalism, creativity, and attention to detail brought this story to life with grace and precision. Your thoughtful guidance ensured every page carried the warmth, clarity, and compassion that this story was meant to share. Your dedication to preserving the book's emotional truth while enhancing its readability made an immeasurable difference. I am deeply grateful for your care, patience, and commitment to excellence throughout this journey.

Finally to everyone who works tirelessly in the pursuit of cures: May God bless your efforts and guide your hands and hearts toward healing.

– Monika

Hi I'm Brooklyn

I live with my mama, papa, and little brother Jacob.

when I was first born, I was mama and papa's only child. we did everything together!

When baby Jacob was born, I loved having a little brother. I helped mama by getting him toys and taking care of him. As Jacob grew older, he sometimes got into my things and messed up my room, but we were still a happy family.

One day, when Jacob was two, he got a bad tummy ache. Mama and papa took him to the hospital, and the doctors said he had cancer.

Everything changed.

Jacob was sick. Mama and papa had to rush him to the hospital all the time for things like blood transfusions, platelet infusions, and chemotherapy — WHATEVER ALL THAT MEANS! Jacob had something called a "port." Mama said it was used to give him his medicine.

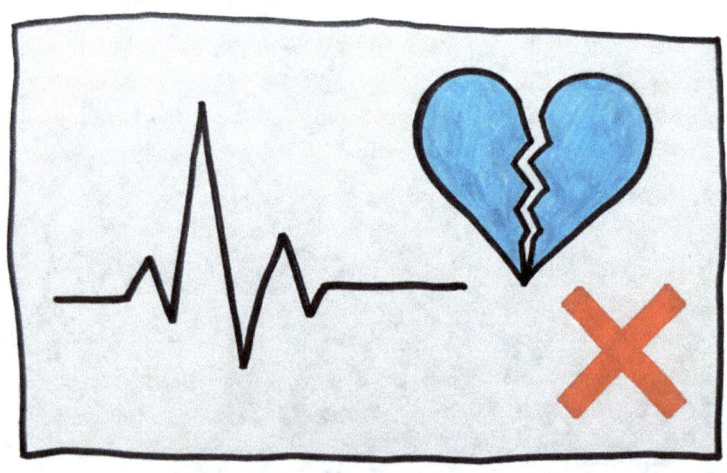

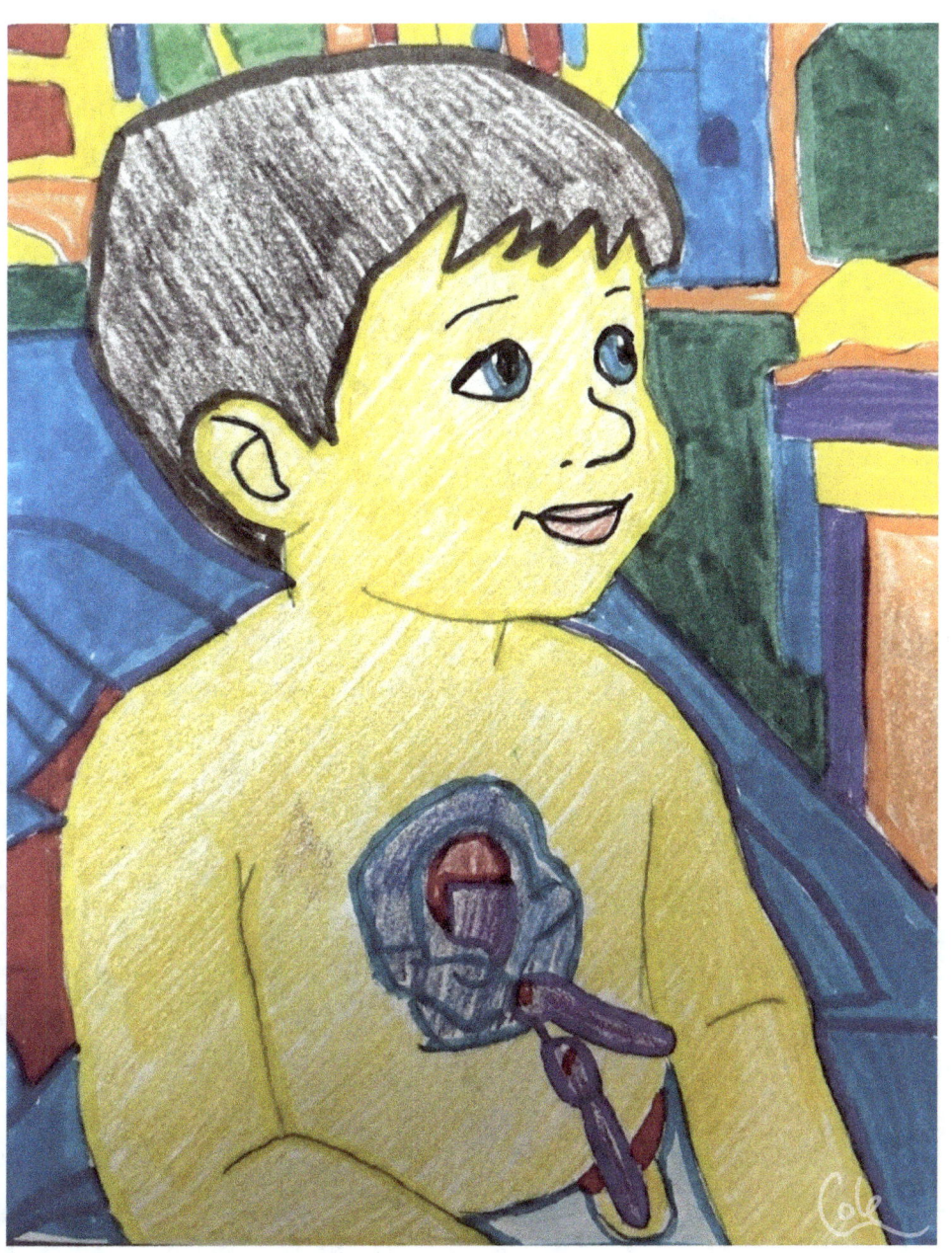

I was upset. Everyone was worried about Jacob. No one seemed to pay attention to me.

I felt lonely, scared, forgotten – AND MAD. It was like I wasn't even there.

17

My grandparents came to help, and I
stayed with them most of the time.

But I missed my mama and papa.

It made me feel better to go to my room and play in my closet with the door closed, or under the bed, or in my special "Brooklyn places." One day my GG came to sit with me in my tent and asked me what I was thinking.

I told her that I didn't understand why the doctors couldn't take care of Jacob while mama and papa took care of me.

It felt good to tell her how I was feeling.

My GG worked with the nice people at the cancer hospital and made me a "Coping Basket."

It had pictures of special treats for me to pick when I was sad. The treats were things like: making cookies, going to a movie, going out to dinner, or getting a new book. It really helped.

It took a long time, but Jacob
is finally better.

we are a happy, healthy
family again.

I love my little brother, and even
though he still gets into my things,
he's my best friend.

It's me, Brooklyn, with my little brother Jacob!
He's my best friend. I love him so much!